Basic Domestic Pet Library

Rabbits Today
A Complete and Up-to-Date Guide

Approved by the ASPCA

Horst Schmidt

Published in association with T.F.H. Publications, Inc.,
the world's largest and most respected publisher of pet literature

Chelsea House Publishers
Philadelphia

Basic Domestic Pet Library
A Cat in the Family
Amphibians Today
Aquarium Beautiful
Choosing the Perfect Cat
Dog Obedience Training
Dogs: Selecting the Best Dog for You
Ferrets Today
Guppies Today
Hamsters Today
Housebreaking and Training Puppies
Iguanas in Your Home
Kingsnakes & Milk Snakes
Kittens Today
Lovebirds Today
Parakeets Today
Pot-bellied Pigs
Rabbits Today
Turtles Today

Publisher's Note: All of the photographs in this book have been coated with FOTOGLAZE™ finish, a special lamination that imparts a new dimension of colorful gloss to the photographs.

Reinforced Library Binding & Super-Highest Quality Boards

This edition © 1997 T.F.H. Publications, Inc., 1 TFH Plaza, Neptune City, NJ 07753. This special library bound edition is made expressly for Chelsea House Publishers, a division of Main Line Book Company.

1 3 5 7 9 8 6 4 2

Library of Congress Cataloging-in-Publication Data

Schmidt, Horst.
    Rabbits Today: a complete and up-to-date guide / Horst Schmidt.
        p. cm. -- (Basic domestic pet library)
    "Approved by the ASPCA"
    Includes index.
    ISBN 0-7910-4617-6 (hardcover)
1. Rabbits.
I. American Society for the Prevention of Cruelty to Animals.
II. Title. III. Series.
SF453.S42 1997
636.9'322--dc21

97-3632
CIP

RABBITS

by Horst Schmidt

yearBOOK

yearBOOKS, INC.
Glen S. Axelrod
Chief Executive Officer

Gary Hersch
Executive Vice President

Barry Duke
Chief Operating Officer

Marilee Talman
Editor-in-Chief

Todd Kelly
Editor

DIGITAL PRE-PRESS
Patricia Northrup
Supervisor

Robert Onyrscuk
Jose Reyes
Digital Pre-Press Production

COMPUTER ART
Patti Escabi
Candida Moreira
Joanne Muzyka

ADVERTISING SALES
Nancy S. Rivadeneira
Advertising Sales Director
Cheryl J. Blyth
Chris O' Brien
Advertising Account Managers
Adrienne Rescinio
Advertising Production Manager
Frances Wrona
Advertising Coordinator

©yearBOOKS, Inc.
1 TFH Plaza
Neptune, N.J. 07753
Completely manufactured in Neptune, N.J.
USA

Photography by: David Robinson, Isabelle Francais, Robert Pearcy, Bruce Crook, Michael Gilroy and Ray Hanson.

Rabbits are interesting pets because they are curious about their environment and respond quickly to stimuli. They are among the most popular domestic pets today and are a favorite for people of all ages. At first glance, people become fascinated with rabbits because they are cute and cuddly. While this is undeniably true, rabbits have many advantages as pets. If they are cared for properly, they are very easy to tame, make no noise and do not give off unpleasant odors. Special thanks to Bob Bennett, Darlene Campbell, U. Erich Friese and Marcy Myerovich for their contributions.

What are yearBOOKS?

Because keeping Rabbits as pets is growing at a rapid pace, information on their selection, care and breeding is vitally needed in the marketplace. Books, the usual way information of this sort is transmitted, can be too slow. Sometimes by the time a book is written and published, the material contained therein is a year or two old...and no new material has been added during that time. Only a book in a magazine form can bring breaking stories and current information. A magazine is streamlined in production, so we have adopted certain magazine publishing techniques in the creation of this yearBOOK. Magazines also can be much cheaper than books because they are supported by advertising. To combine these assets into a great publication, we issued this yearBOOK in both magazine and book format at different prices.

CONTENTS

Rabbits are extremely
easy pets to care for.

EVOLUTION OF THE RABBIT

The rabbit has not only provided man with food, clothing, and sport, but also has managed to survive and multiply under some adverse circumstances. When the rabbit became domesticated is unclear, but several sources have been documented. One such authority states that wild rabbits were first kept caged in Africa, while another suggests that domestication began during the Middle Ages by French monks who kept them in captivity and bred them. It is known that as early as 3000 years ago, the rabbit was an important source of food in Asian and European countries.

Nearly all history accounts dealing with the rabbit mention Spain. Caves in Spain dating back to the Stone Age contain colored pictures of rabbits, indicating that the rabbit was important to man during this period. Rabbits have an ancient fossil record, making them among the most ancient of living mammals of Europe, as well as America. Some fossils date back 30 to 40 million years. A sphinx located in Turkey and dating back to 1500 B.C. is standing on the figures of two rabbits.

In early times, the rabbit was prized mainly as a food source. Around 250 B.C., the Romans encouraged the spread of wild rabbits for hunting. However, due to the animal being so easily adapted to its surroundings, the project backfired. The rabbit was so fertile that it proved impossible to control its numbers via hunting.

The Portuguese promoted the rabbit as a source of fresh meat on long journeys and experienced the same population difficulties also. Around 1418, Porto Santo (of the Madeira Islands) was overrun by rabbits. The Portuguese had introduced the rabbit to the island, but it multiplied at such a fast rate and to such an extent that the island had to be abandoned. It was no longer habitable by people.

The rabbit was introduced into Australia in modern times to provide game for sportsmen, only to have the project end with tragic consequences. European rabbits were set free in Australian public parks and, having no natural enemies, they prospered to the extent of competing with herds of livestock for food. The rabbits consumed the grass together with its roots, they debarked bushes and trees, and endangered sheep breeding in the states of Victoria, South Australia, and Queensland. In order to bring the rabbit population under control, predators (such as ferrets) were introduced. More drastic measures had to be taken, and an infectious disease, myxomatosis, was deliberately introduced. Finally, a campaign to destroy the remaining rabbit population on the continent was initiated through the use of poisons.

Another example of the rabbit adapting to its environment was revealed in the late 1800s, when rabbits were released on a group of islands near the South Pole. They were to provide meat for whale hunters and teams of researchers living on the islands. In spite of the sub-zero temperatures during the winter and the total lack of vegetation, the rabbits

> **"The ancient Aztecs also held the rabbit in esteem for the flavor and quality of its meat."**

managed to survive by eating seaweed that drifted ashore.

The Romans, while occupying Spain, discovered how to keep the rabbit population under control by raising colonies of them in walled rabbit yards and guarded sheds. The meat was considered a delicacy and it was believed to contribute to the beauty of a woman. At that time, rabbits were also being established on some Mediterranean islands. The ancient Aztecs also held the rabbit in esteem for the flavor and quality of its meat. Court physicians prescribed it as an effective body rebuilder, even though they did not realize the scientific value of proteins, carbohydrates, fats, minerals, and vitamins, or that rabbit meat contained these necessary elements for good health in greater degree than did other meats.

The American Indian hunted the wild rabbit in early times, but exactly when the domestic rabbit was introduced in the United States is not known. Since Europeans, notably the French, were fond of rabbit meat, it is believed that the domestic rabbit was brought into the United States well before 1900. Early attempts to establish rabbits in the United States failed or became very expensive. In Ohio, Pennsylvania, and New York only 1,600 rabbits were killed by hunters from the 20,000 that were released. The reduction of rabbit numbers was probably due to the many natural enemies which were originally absent in Australia.

Americans became rabbit-raising conscious around the turn of the century with the

Rabbits have played a role in European folklore. They are notably associated with the arrival of spring.

importation of the Belgian Hare, which is not a hare at all, but a rabbit. It was imported from England, and Americans realized that this productive animal was an asset to agriculture.

Rabbitries began springing up across the country, with Los Angeles having more and larger rabbitries than anywhere else in the country. Los Angeles continued to be the major area for rabbit production and processing for many years, and today it still ranks high. This could be due in part to the large numbers of ethnic groups that consider rabbit a major part in their diet.

The Belgian Hare, with its blockier body than is bred for today and its rapid rate of reproduction, caught the eye of the rabbit raising public. Thus, a new industry was created.

During World War II, when meat was rationed and extremely difficult to get, rabbit raisers found an eager market for the litters that they could produce in their backyards. People with a few hutches of rabbits soon had a money-making business.

Today, rabbits are raised throughout the United States as well as in some U.S. owned territories. There over 40 breeds of rabbit from which you can choose, with numerous varieties within each breed. Most breeds serve a dual purpose. That of meat and fur, or commercial and fancy. Anyone developing an interest in rabbits can be assured that the rabbit has been of prime importance to man since the earliest recorded time.

Despite adverse circumstances and periodic attempts at extinction, it has survived and flourished and will continue on. The rabbit has provided man with a variety of commodities, including meat, pelts, wool, and various by-products. Additionally, it has played an important role in medical research.

During World War II, when meat was rationed and extremely difficult to get, rabbit raisers found an eager market for the litters that they could produce in their backyards.

THE PROPER CARE OF YOUR RABBIT

Rabbits up until the age of eight weeks should be with their mother at all times.

Once you bring home your new pet rabbit, you have immediately taken responsibility for a live animal. If it's caged, as it probably is most of the time, it is totally dependent upon you. If it is loose in your yard, it is still almost as dependent because your rabbit is a domesticated animal, not a wild one. It does not have the keen instinct and defenses of a wild rabbit. It does not have a sense of fear resulting from experiences in the wild. And it probably can't run or hop as fast as its wild cousin.

Your first responsibility is to feed your rabbit correctly–to nourish what is probably a young and growing animal. Your second responsibility is to house your pet comfortably and safely.

If you obtain a rabbit, but are awaiting to have the proper food and housing, the first thing you should do is not feed the rabbit greens. A dish of fresh, clean water and perhaps some dry bread will do if you do not have any real rabbit pellets. Make sure that the housing accommodations have proper ventilation. You can lay down the floor with straw, shavings, or even torn strips of crumpled newspaper. This will keep the rabbit dry and comfortable until you get the proper setup. Make sure no other domestic pets can get at him. If these measures are taken, the rabbit will be fine provided you get the proper housing from a nearby petshop the following day.

There are several considerations to take into account when choosing the type of housing that is just right for your rabbit. It is vital that your rabbit's accommodations are large enough so that your pet can move about in complete comfort. Naturally, the size of your rabbit will determine the size of his

> **"Naturally, the size of your rabbit will determine the size of his house, but even the smallest breed of rabbit should have accommodations that allow it to move about freely."**

house, but even the smallest breed of rabbit should have accommodations that allow it to move about freely.

Whatever type of housing that you choose for your rabbit, it should be durable and easy to maintain. Wire cages have much to offer in this respect. They are more sturdier than wood and can better withstand a rabbit's gnawing. Another important feature of the wire cage is that it comes equipped with a pull-out tray on the bottom. The droppings that collect in the

tray can be disposed of easily.

Whether indoors or outdoors, your rabbit's housing should be located in an area that is well ventilated. The location should be bright, but you should also afford your pet the opportunity to retreat to the shade when the weather is hot. If outdoors, your rabbit's house must be protected from the elements and from predators.

Besides food and shelter, it may be a good idea to invest in other equipment for your rabbit. You need either a feed crock or a hopper feeder. Both are readily available at your local pet store. The crock should be heavy crockery, not plastic. Rabbits will eat plastic dishes. Since plastic is lightweight, your rabbit could tip it over and waste the feed. Investing in a good heavy crock for feed will conserve money in saved feed. The best ones have a "lip" inside at the top to prevent the rabbit from scratching the feed out and wasting it.

Cages made of wire are a good investment because they are less subject to damage potentially caused by a rabbit.

A hopper feeder is made of galvanized iron. You fasten it to the front of the hutch, which lets you feed the rabbit without opening the hutch door. If you use a hopper feeder, you should not fill it up, but measure the correct amount of pellets for your pet and pour them in. If you

Although the rabbit myth suggests the use of carrots, keep in mind that giving your rabbit variety in its diet is essential.

are away for an extended period of time, a hopper feeder allows you to put in extra feed, which descends from the hopper to the trough section as your rabbit eats. It is a feature that makes the hopper feeder a popular choice.

The first choice for watering equipment in warm weather is the plastic water bottle with the stainless steel stem. These are widely available and should be in your pet store. The larger the size, usually about a quart, the better. On a hot day, your pet rabbit will be able to just about empty it. The water bottle is ideal because all you need to do is put the water in and seal it up. The water will stay clean and doesn't take up any space on the hutch floor. Obviously, the water bottle will not work below freezing temperatures. This is when you use a water crock or a metal water pan.

If you use a crock, be sure to examine the inside of it

carefully before you buy one. The bottom should be narrower than the top on the inside. That way, if the water freezes the ice will slide up. Water expands when it freezes, so if the ice has nowhere to go but against the walls of the crock, you will wind up with a broken crock. It is important to mention again to avoid plastic–the rabbit will eat it. A metal pan is useful in the winter because when the water freezes you can pop the ice out of the pan by hitting hit against a hard surface. Or you may simply dip it into a pail of warm water to thaw it and slip the ice out.

Water your rabbit at least twice a day during cold weather. Rabbits will not survive if all he has for water is ice to lick. It is convenient during cold weather to own two watering crocks or pans. Be sure to keep one inside where it's warm to thaw so at watering time you don't have the problem of frozen crocks.

With a little creativity and added costs, you can avoid

"You could electrocute your rabbit if you improperly put electric heat tape around the water crock."

the problem of frozen water. Immersion heaters such as ones used in bird baths are suitable. Electric heat tape could be wrapped around your water crock, provided the tape is protected from rabbits gnawing on it. You could electrocute your rabbit if you fail to do this right.

Rabbits always want to find something to do, so you need to give your pet as much attention as you can. Rabbits can be entertained quite easily. You can provide it with a couple of small tin cans for the rabbit to toss and roll them around. A stick or a branch from a fruit tree can be very appealing. A box top to hop on or over is fun for your rabbit as well.

Cramped living quarters can cause stress, which can lower a rabbit's resistance to illness.

Regardless of what type of rabbit you keep, it will make a great pet for everyone in the household.

RESPONSIBILITY FOR YOU AND YOUR RABBIT

Hopefully, a rabbit that is properly cared for will enjoy a good state of health. Many of the illnesses that strike rabbits are the result of unsanitary living conditions, improper care, or poor diet. Good husbandry is very important in keeping your rabbit healthy. Make sure the cage tray is emptied daily and clean the entire cage once a week. Also remember to remove uneaten food daily.

Much of the enjoyment of having a rabbit for a pet is being able to pick him up, pet him, hold him, and carry him about. There are ways of going about it that both you and he will appreciate.

Feed your rabbit pellets made especially for them.

touch the rabbit and contact your veterinarian or ask a local petshop for a liquid medication that can be administered.

Most owners aren't as concerned with what a rabbit can get as they do about what they might get from the rabbit. Rabbits don't need any shots, and they don't get rabies or distemper. They are generally very healthy pets. With proper housing and feeding of your rabbit, you will be avoiding many potential problems.

Unfortunately, even with the best of care, rabbits can become ill. Stomach disorders can be serious, sometimes even fatal, and should be treated as soon as they are detected. A rabbit that has diarrhea should be taken off all greenfoods immediately

First, think of yourself. Rabbits have sharp toenails, especially young ones. They can also shed their fur on occasion. Furthermore, while they are usually very careful, sometimes a rabbit can have an accident while you are holding him, and your clothing may be affected. Therefore, it's a good idea to wear something of a good, sturdy material to wear while handling the rabbit.

Now, think of your rabbit. Picking him up and playing with him should be an enjoyable experience for him. You obviously would not want to hurt him. There are several ways to handle rabbits.

The important aspect to bear in mind is to pick up the rabbit in such a way that he feels comfortable and secure. Never pick him up by the ears, and always support him under either the hindquarters or the chest–not the stomach! If he feels comfortable and secure, he will not struggle or kick and scratch. Should he do this, it will be no fun for either of you.

You should know that you can't catch anything from your rabbit with the exception of ringworm. Ringworm is caused by a parasite and is indicated by circular patches of fur falling out. Rarely does this occur, but should it happen, do not

> **"Ringworm is caused by a parasite and is indicated by circular patches of fur falling out."**

Your local petshop can provide you with a nutritionally complete rabbit food for your pet.

and given an anti-diarrheal preparation. Some experienced rabbit keepers regularly treat their stock with sulfaquinoxaline as a preventative against coccidiosis, a digestive tract infection that is not uncommon in rabbits.

There may be problems encountered that you may cause. Perhaps you house more than one rabbit to a hutch that contains another adult rabbit, the mother may not care for the young, she may even kill them. The first thing to remember is that every rabbit needs its own hutch. Two or more adults in a single hutch is asking for a problem that will cause you tremendous headaches.

The way to go about avoiding more problems is to do certain precautions. First, rabbit. Check for the bright eyes, the glossy coat, and make sure your rabbit is active. If your rabbit is a "thumper," give him a board to stomp on.

Your pet store may carry sulfaquinoxaline sodium. If it doesn't, your local feed and grain store will. If you can't find it, you can send away for it by writing to a supplier listed in a rabbit magazine.

Some rabbits can get along with other family pets. The introduction should be made gradually.

cage. This is not recommended because if they are mature rabbits and they are both males, they will tend to fight. If you house two females, the possibility of fighting exists, but it is not as great. If you house one of each gender, you will wind up with an event you didn't expect. This latter case is perhaps the worst thing you could do. A mother rabbit needs extra feed and a nesting box, and she needs her own hutch. If baby rabbits are produced in a maintain a regular feeding schedule with rabbit pellets. Never give greens to young rabbits. It also helps to keep the water fresh and pure. Rinse the crocks and bottles daily. Keep a close eye on your Sulfaquinoxaline sodium comes in a bottle. A pint of the concentrate should last about a year and is reasonably priced. Usually, the drug is diluted with drinking water and given for two days in a

> **"Two or more adults in a single hutch is asking for a problem that will cause you tremendous headaches."**

row, withheld for another two days, and given for two more days on a monthly basis. Sulfaquinoxaline sodium prevents coccidiosis.

Coccidiosis is the most common infection of domestic rabbits. It can stunt the growth or perhaps kill young rabbits. The symptoms of coccidiosis include diarrhea, a bloated belly, and generally poor condition indicated by a lack of gloss and general roughness of the fur. A parasite causes coccidiosis.

Your rabbit should not develop ear mites if you keep it in a wire cage. Ear mites are parasites as well. Before the parasite finds a host, they live in manure. If the rabbit lives in a wire cage, he does not come into contact with the manure and as a result, will not contract ear mites. Should ear mites occur in a rabbit, they are very easy to cure. There will be scabby encrustations inside the ears. Simply pour in a little mineral oil and you will drown them. It might take a few applications.

Art. # 61230   Art. # 61231   Art. # 61232

Absorbent and inexpensive pine bedding material is readily available at petshops. Photo courtesy of Hagen.

You should put in about half a teaspoonful. An eye or nose dropper is a good applicator.

Another problem that occasionally occurs in rabbits is sore hocks. This is when rabbit's hind foot or feet become ulcerated, perhaps from stomping on a wire cage floor. Give your rabbit a resting board to get his feet off the wire floor. Mild cases can be treated with iodine or an antibiotic ointment. If the condition persists, take the rabbit to your veterinarian. When you pick your rabbit up, look him over, including his feet.

There are other problems that may not really be big problems, but can be easily noticed. Such is the case with flies. If flies surround your rabbit hutch, remove the manure regularly from the cage. Flies breed in manure. If manure is not present, then the flies won't be either. This problem is obviously not a factor during cold weather. Another problem to watch for is that of mice. You won't have any mice around should you feed your rabbits only the amount of feed they can eat in a day and keep the pellet supply in a metal container with a tight lid. If you leave a bag of pellets lying around outdoors or in the garage, you will attract mice.

Rabbits like these Netherland Dwarfs are among the most popular breeds of rabbit.

RABBITS AND CHILDREN

People of all ages own and enjoy rabbits, but children especially are easily captivated by these charming, lovable pets. In general, rabbit care is not difficult, and a child can actively participate in caring for the family's pet rabbit.

It is not a bad idea to have adult supervision when children are around rabbits early on.

For children, the main motive to keep animals is the fascination of looking after a living being. A domestic pet brings joy in all humans, especially then when it conforms in shape, color, and behavior to a certain scheme. Animals which have short, round heads with a high forehead, large eyes, stub noses and short ears, a compact body, short limbs, awkward movements and soft fur are certainly preferred by humans over beings with long

People of all ages enjoy rabbits, but children are especially curious by their lovable nature.

additional reasons to justify the keeping of pets by children.

All aspects, such as the need for play, natural partnerships, and biological interest, must be converted to responsible hands-on animal care when species are selected which by their nature are suitable for keeping as a pet Unfortunately, this is not always the case with species which are kept indoors, on a balcony, or in the yard. On the other hand, there are animals in which a child's care is not always the ideal pet, despite its "children characteristics."

Animals, with which children can come into direct contact by

faces, large ears, and angular shapes. Very young children will need to be taught the correct way to handle their bunny rabbit. Adult supervision is a good idea when a young child and his pet play together.

> **"...children will need to be taught the correct way to handle their bunny rabbit."**

In older children and adolescents, there are additional requirements. The care and maintenance of animals provides a high degree of satisfaction, in as much as the young person gains the experience that other creatures can become a sort of "animal partner." Here, it need not be stressed that such educational objectives in this day and age of increasing alienation from nature and advancing technology must also be maintained in the keeping of domestic and pet animals.

Recognizing species-specific types of behavior, rearing of young, and the progress of development are

Rabbits enjoy being picked up and handled.

touching and petting them are more the exception rather than the rule in the large spectrum of domestic animals. Small birds, aquarium fishes, and terrarium animals are not "contact animals." Dogs and cats can go a long way towards fulfilling the child's need for direct contact with the animal as a friend. However, dogs show little original behavior which is

> **"In choosing to keep rabbits, you can find a pleasant pastime and rewarding hobby."**

undesirable from the human point of view and cats tend to keep themselves away from contact of children. In contrast to the typical needs of young people and in respect to other animal species, the dwarf rabbit is virtually ideal as a "partner animal." It is superbly adapted to the child's needs, the educational objectives from the parents point of view, and to the traits of the animal itself.

For many rabbit hobbyists, rabbits have uses far beyond that of their commercial value. They are delightful pets and are also a means of teaching animal husbandry to youngsters. The most important ingredient in raising rabbits is a liking for animals. In choosing to keep rabbits, you can find a pleasant pastime and rewarding hobby.

Make sure your children know the proper procedure to picking up a rabbit.

While rabbits are very adaptable to changes, they need consistent care and attention to be a happy pet.

AVAILABILITY AND SUITABILITY

The biggest decision that you will have to make when selecting your pet rabbit is in choosing a breed that will be suitable for you and your family. Naturally, personal preference will play a major role, but there are several factors that must be considered before you make your final choice.

The "coat" of the rabbit is one consideration in making your selection. Some breeds have fur coats that are short and dense. Other breeds have coats that are long and wooly. If you want one of these wooly breeds, will you or someone in your family groom it on a regular basis? If you are interested in any of the lop-eared breeds, keep in mind that their ears will need extra attention. Loppy ears can be prone to parasitic infestation. Additionally, they are more subject to injuries such as scratches and cuts.

Never purchase a rabbit that is under two months of age. Although some baby rabbits are taken away from their mothers at less than this age and they survive, their optimal early development is not as good as rabbits that remain with their mothers for a whole two months. When you examine your prospective rabbit, gently stroke it along the back and sides. If the spine and ribs are easily felt, then the animal is likely underweight and should not be considered for purchase.

It is essential that you select a rabbit that looks well fed and hops around animatedly. You should avoid one that huddles in a corner of the pen away from the others. Look for an inquisitive rabbit with bright eyes and a dry nose. Check the insides of the forelegs. If the fur is stuck together, it is a sign that the rabbit has a cold. Rabbits with colds tend to wipe their noses with the inside of their front paws and legs.

You should also want to examine its front teeth. The uppers and lowers should come together evenly, or mesh. If the uppers and lowers overlap significantly, the rabbit has malocclusion or "buck teeth" or "wolf teeth." Since rabbits' teeth grow continuously and must be ground down constantly by chewing, they must meet evenly. Otherwise, they will continue to grow and prevent the rabbit from eating. Malocclusion ordinarily is a congenital defect, although some rabbits will pull their teeth out of alignment by chewing on their cages.

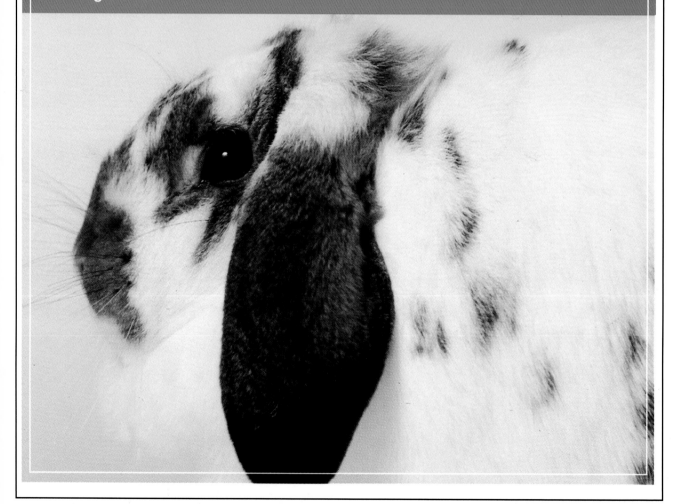

Lop rabbits are covered with dense wool on their bodies, but the ears are coated with regular fur.

It is also important to check the ears. Look down inside them to make certain there are no crusty brown scales that would indicate ear mites. If the ears are clean, pick out a male if it is possible since males "buck" generally make better pets than females "doe," which often may not have a pleasant disposition.

In general, the average lifespan of domestic rabbits is about six to eight years of age, but there are records of rabbits that have lived up to twelve or more years. Female rabbits that have not been mated tend to be the longest living rabbits.

The following summarizes the most important points about the question of suitability:

1.) It is completely domesticated. The rabbit can adapt to accommodations in the house.
2.) It has a "peaceful character." The rabbit is not aggressive towards small children and will not bite them.
3.) It is relatively undemanding in respect to accommodation, size of the enclosure, and food.
4.) It is clean and does not give off an odor when kept properly.
5.) It has a highly interesting behavior, especially during reproduction and rearing of young.
6.) It has little danger of disease transmission in comparison to other domesticated animals.
7.) It can recognize their keeper and they like to maintain direct contact.

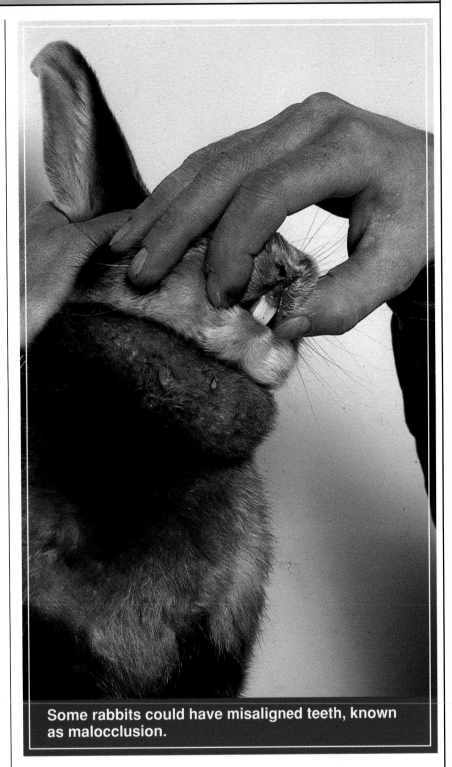

Some rabbits could have misaligned teeth, known as malocclusion.

They like to be petted without becoming "imprinted" or losing their natural types of behavior.
8.) It can correspond closely to the "children scheme."

Of course, these "advantages" are valid only if all other prerequisites in regard to acquisition, maintenance, care, and diet are being complied.

Rabbits lend themselves to calm and quiet captivity. They never become overly excited.

ANALYZING BEHAVIOR OF DOMESTICATED RABBITS

The genetic origin of the pet rabbit was the European wild rabbit. This is an extremely active, mobile and relatively intelligent animal, which lives in large aggregations which have a well-defined social structure. The relationship between the sexes as well as that between parents and their young and also that among juvenile rabbits is precisely regulated by instincts. This has been researched and subsequently documented by ethologists in considerable detail.

When we observe our dwarf rabbits to suddenly race off in wild, oblique jumps with sudden directional changes, this is behavior which came originally from its wild ancestors. Their progeny initially performs this flight behavior as a sort of play, until it becomes a genuine survival technique.

Wild male rabbits "mark" their territory with a scent given off by special chin and anal glands. Our tame pet rabbit will do the same, preferably on the legs of furniture. Do not worry about this, for there is virtually no odor. Even wild female rabbits are marked by courting males simply by urinating at them. Should this possibly happen from a male pet rabbit, it is only a sign of affection!

Let's examine a specific behavior in rabbits which could you could draw some conclusions when you observe your domestic rabbit. Foot stomping, or thumping, is very common in rabbits. This is used to express threats and to ward off potential enemies. A herd of rabbits interprets this as a warning signal, especially those animals which have not yet noticed the source of intrusion.

Although much of your pet rabbit's original behavior has been removed, deliberately or inadvertently through selective breeding, they have retained certain basic biological requirements and instinctive behavior. These must be taken into consideration when rabbits are kept as pets.

First of all, it is important to recognize the rabbit's expressions with which it indicates moods and needs. When our pet emits short, almost barking growls, it indicates an aggressive mood

> **"Although much of your rabbit's behavior has been removed, deliberately or inadvertently through selective breeding, they have retained certain basic biological requirements and instinctive behavior."**

often followed by a biting or scratching attack. When a rabbit is held on the arm, it sometimes vocalizes with chirping sounds. The rabbit would rather be put down and run on the floor. The proverbial teeth grinding in rabbits is a sign that they feel comfortable and relaxed.

When a male rabbit is kept as a family pet, it can sometimes be seen encircle its human companions bringing leaves, twigs or bits of paper and and emitting a soft humming noise. This type of behavior certainly has its origin in the species-specific courting, whereby the male brings nesting material to the female.

When rabbits are excited, their body posture becomes tense and the small tails is held erect. When they are ready to attack, the ears are held back against the body. When the animals are kept in a large garden enclosure or in an apartment, it is common to observe the rabbits marking their territory with the underside of the chin, where the scent glands are located. By doing this, the animals establish "scent paths," but these cannot be perceived by the human sense of smell. The animals tend to frequent these paths regularly. Similarly, the animals' favorite spot always serves as the center of the territory, where the animals are most comfortable. This can be seen from the position of the extended abdomen, which expresses the need for rest and sleep.

One question frequently asked in respect to typical rabbit behavior is can a rabbit be raised like a pet dog. It can because there can be no specific training or conditioned response. However, some of the training starts right at the beginning of the adaptation phase. Usually, a rabbit is bought very young, when it was still part of the original litter. Then it is suddenly taken into different surroundings and feels separated from its siblings. The first bond that the animal re-establishes is with its new home. It should be left alone for a few days, so that it can absorb the scent and appearance of its new surroundings and then adjust to it.

Then gradually a few choice tidbits are offered cautiously so that the animal gets used to the human hand and it will soon gain confidence. When taken on to your lap it will feel the pleasant warmth and then permit you to pet it. Once the animal has a free run of surroundings, the "rabbit toilet" with absorbent litter is also set up. The animal is placed on this tray several times during the day, so that it gets used to it and does not start to use some other corner to defecate your home. Most animals will learn this surprisingly fast, but it would be totally wrong to use "punishment methods."

It's advised not to put a rabbit on a leash. Although the animals will learn to some degree to tolerate the little chest harness, they are finding it difficult to cope with being walked like a dog. The locomotary apparatus of rabbits alone

" A rabbit would never accept a human as the lead animal."

prohibits jerking pulls or extreme body movements caused by the leash. In fact, it would be cruel to prompt the rabbit to walk like a dog. A rabbit would never accept a human as the lead animal.

Netherland dwarfs come in a variety of colors.

There are over 40
breeds of rabbits to
choose from.

VARIOUS BREEDS

Probably the toughest decision that you will have to make is in selecting the one rabbit breed that is most suitable for you. Each breed has its own unique charm and appeal. The best thing for you to do is to first decide what you want from your rabbit. Is the animal to be a pet or to be exhibited? Are you interested in breeding it later on? Once you answer these questions, your process in selecting a rabbit will be made much easier.

Another major consideration is fur type. Rabbit breeds fall into one of four distinct fur, or coat, types. The fur type is the basis for the first basic difference between rabbit breeds.

The fur common to most rabbits and most familiar to the average person is classified as normal. The characteristic dominant coat has an undercoat protect by longer protective guard hairs.

An Angora coat is a long coat of wool-type fiber, making it excellent for spinning and weaving.

A mutation of the normal coat is known as a Rex coat.

There is no such thing as a "best rabbit breed." The one that the hobbyist feels is most appealing is probably the one best suited to him. Be sure to purchase the best rabbit you can afford. It will be much easier to care for a healthy, well-conditioned rabbit than one that is not in a state of good health.

The following descriptions are of breeds recognized by

front of the hip joint. Overall, the American appears compact. It is a rabbit of medium bone and medium weight.

AMERICAN FUZZY LOP

Groups: Agouti, Broken, Pointed White, Self, Shaded, and Solid

Colors: Agouti–Chestnut, Chinchilla, Lynx, Opal, Squirrel; Broken–any recognized breed color along with White and exhibiting the breed pattern; Pointed White–White body with the points of any recognized color; Self–Black, Blue, Chocolate, Lilac; Self (Blue-Eyed Whites and Ruby Eyed Whites)–White; Shaded–Sable Point, Siamese Sable, Siamese Smoke Pearl, Tortoiseshell; Solid–Fawn, Orange

Weight: Bucks and Does, not over 4 pounds

The Fuzzy Lop exhibits a body that is cobby and short in appearance. Beginning at the shoulders, there should be good depth that continues back to the hindquarters, which should be well filled and well rounded. The head is set high and close to the shoulders. The Fuzzy Lop is a wool-breed rabbit. Its wool should be dense, and the density is even throughout the entire body.

You should choose a rabbit with a nice full coat and no bare patches.

This type of fur is shorter and more plush in texture than is normal fur. The guard hairs are reduced in length so as to be nearly the length of the undercoat, presenting a level appearance to the coat. Rex fur is very luxurious to the touch.

A Satin coat is characterized by the fine hair shafts. The hair shells, which are more transparent than those of normal-furred rabbits, reflect light. A Satin coat exhibits a beautiful satin-like sheen.

the ARBA. Individual clubs are located around the country to support specific breeds and varieties. These clubs are an excellent means of exchanging information and ideas among rabbit keepers.

AMERICAN

Varieties: Blue and white
Weight: Bucks 9 to 11 pounds; Does 10 to 12 pounds

The body of the American should exhibit a moderate arch which begins at the shoulders and reaches its high point in the area just in

AMERICAN SABLE

Color: Rich sepia brown on the ears, face, back and outside of legs, and the upper side of the tail. Saddle color will consistently gradate to a paler tone on the flanks and the underside of the belly and tail.

Weight: Bucks 7 to 9 pounds; Does 8 to 10 pounds

The body is to be of

ABOVE: The American Fuzzy Lop is one of the newer breeds of rabbit. BELOW: One distinguishing feature of the American Sable is how its eyes exhibit a ruby-red glow when viewed in reflected light.

(Blue-Eyed Whites and Red-Eyed Whites)–White; Colored–Agouti, Chestnut, Chinchilla, Chocolate Agouti, Chocolate Chinchilla, Copper, Lilac Chinchilla, Lynx, Opal, Squirrel, Wild Gray; Self–Black, Blue, Chocolate, Lilac; Shaded–Blue Cream, Chocolate Tortoiseshell, Dark Sable, Frosted Pearl, Lilac Cream, Sable, Smoke Pearl, Tortoiseshell; Solid-Cream, Fawn, Red; Ticked–Blue Steel, Chocolate Steel, Lilac Steel, Steel

Weight: Bucks 5 to 7 pounds; Does 5 to $7^1/_2$ pounds

The English Angora has a compact, cobby body with a good uniform coat of wool. It has the appearance of a round ball of fluff. The head has heavy bangs and side trimmings, and the ears are heavily tasseled. The legs, feet, and tail are covered with wool to the extreme ends. The wool of this rabbit is silky in nature. It is a wool-producing animal, whereas some other breeds of rabbit are considered to be fur producers.

medium length. There is to be good depth and width in the shoulders as well as the midsection and hindquarters. The American Sable's top line should present itself in an unbroken continuous curve. The hindquarters are to be smooth and well rounded.

ANGORA (ENGLISH)
Groups: Agouti, Pointed White, Self, Shaded, Solid, Ticked

Colors: White with marking color of Black, Blue, Chocolate, or Lilac; Self

The growths of wool on the ears of the English Angora are known as furnishings.

ANGORA (FRENCH)

Groups: Agouti, Pointed White, Self, Shaded, Solid, Ticked

Colors: White (Pointed Whites)–White with marking color of Black, Blue, Chocolate or Lilac; Self (Blue-Eyed Whites and Red-Eyed Whites)–White; Colored–Agouti, Chestnut, Chinchilla, Chocolate Agouti, Chocolate Chinchilla, Copper, Lilac Chinchilla, Lynx, Opal, Squirrel, Wild Gray; Self–Black, Blue, Chocolate, Lilac; Shaded–Blue Cream, Chocolate Tortoiseshell, Dark Sable, Frosted Pearl, Lilac Cream, Sable, Smoke Pearl, Tortoiseshell; Solid–Cream, Fawn, Red; Ticked–Blue Steel, Chocolate Steel, Lilac Steel, Steel

Weight: Bucks and Does, $7^{1}/_{2}$ pounds to $10^{1}/_{2}$ pounds

This breed is older that the English Angora and is the commercial wool-producing rabbit. A coarse-textured wool grows to an ideal length of $2^{1}/_{2}$ to $3^{1}/_{2}$ inches. The body is medium in length with a full chest. It is longer and heavier in bone that the English variety. The head is longer and narrower than the English and does not have the heavy bangs and tassels. The tail is covered with wool, but the feet and legs are short-

The ear length of the French Angora should be proportional to that of the head and body.

furred to the first joint. The ears may be tufted, but not tasseled.

ANGORA (GIANT)

Variety: White

Weight: Bucks $8^{1}/_{2}$ pounds and over, Does 9 pounds and over

The Giant Angora should present an overall image of an animal that is well nourished and firmly fleshed. An ideal specimen will be well balanced throughout the body. The

"The Giant Angora should present an overall image of an animal that is well nourished and firmly fleshed."

density of the wool–the greater, the better–is consistently even all over the animal.

ANGORA (SATIN)

Groups: Agouti, Pointed White, Self, Shaded, Solid, Ticked

Colors: White (Pointed Whites)–White with marking color of Black, Blue, Chocolate, or Lilac; Self (Blue-Eyed Whites and Red-Eyed Whites)–White; Colored–Agouti, Chestnut, Chinchilla, Chocolate Agouti, Chocolate

All Angora rabbit owners will need to spend some time brushing and combing the pet's fur.

The Giant Angora is only available in white.

Chinchilla, Copper, Lilac Chinchilla, Lynx, Opal, Squirrel, Wild Gray; Self– Black, Blue, Chocolate, Lilac; Shaded– Blue Cream, Chocolate

> "Beverens are a large breed that produces young that grow rapidly."

Tortoiseshell, Dark Sable, Frosted Pearl, Lilac Cream, Sable, Smoke Pearl, Tortoiseshell; Solid–Cream, Fawn, Red; Ticked–Blue Steel, Chocolate Steel, Lilac Steel, Steel

Weight: Bucks and Does,

BELGIAN HARE
Color: Red chestnut

Weight: Bucks and Does, 6 to 9^1/$_2$ pounds

This breed of rabbit originated in Belgium. Some believe it is descended from an early breed known as the Patagonian (the forefather of the Flemish Giant), which is now extinct. It is the race horse of the rabbit family, with a long, streamlined body and a nicely arched back with

Beveren rabbits have dense and silky fur.

BEVEREN
Varieties: White, Blue, Black

Weight: Bucks 8 to 10 pounds; Does 9 to 11 pounds

The Beveren is one of the rarer breeds in the United States, although it rose in popularity in Europe after its development late in the 19th century.

It is a large breed that produces young that grow rapidly. The body is medium in length and has a meaty back that is slightly arched. The back is full and has good curvature when viewed from the side. The correct color is for the blue to be a clean shade of lavender blue all the way to the skin. The black variety is jet black deep into the fur.

Not only do Belgian Hares show outstanding color, their long legs enable them to move about quickly.

6 pounds or over

The Satin Angora is of medium length with hindquarters that are well filled. The oval head is to be in balance with the body shape and size. The wool of the Satin exhibits a luxuriant richness in color. Glass-like hair shafts permit the reflection of light.

a sweep that runs continuously from the shoulders to the tail. The loin and hindquarters are well rounded. The body is carried well off the ground on long, straight, slender legs. The head is rather long and fine, set on a slender neck. The fur lies close to the body and is of a rather harsh texture.

BRITANNIA PETITE
Color: White

Weight: Bucks and Does, maximum weight of 2^1/$_2$ pounds

Small in stature, but big in spirit aptly describes the Petite. In general appearance, it is slender and fineboned, with an attractive sleek coat. Members of this breed are known for their alert, inquisitive nature and their lively mannerisms.

CALIFORNIAN

Color: White with Black

Weight: Bucks 8 to 10 pounds; Does $8^1/_2$ to 10 pounds

One of the most popular breeds, the Californian was produced for use as an all-purpose commercial rabbit. It excels both as a meat type and a fur type. This is a white rabbit with a colored nose, ears, feet, and tail. The color is to be as black as possible.

The body is very plump and full over the hips, firm and meaty as possible to the nape of the neck and down the sides over the ribs and shoulders.

CHAMPAGNE D'ARGENT

Color: Silver

Weight: Bucks 9 to 11 pounds; Does $9^1/_2$ to 12 pounds

This is one of the oldest rabbit breeds, having been raised in France for over one hundred years. The pelt commands a high price. The name is French for the "silver rabbit from Champagne," the region where the breed originated. The Champagne is both a commercial and exhibition rabbit. The body is moderate in length, and well developed in the hindquarters, shoulders, and back. The most desirable color is that of old silver, or the pale color of skimmed milk with no hint of yellow. The young of this breed are born black and gradually turn to a velvety silver color once past four months of age.

The Britannia Petite is diminutive and known for its inquisitive behavior.

Bear in mind to always house your rabbit separately.

The Champagne D'Argent has a fur color that is like that of old silver.

CHECKERED GIANT (AMERICAN)
Varieties: Black and Blue
Color: Black or blue

markings on a white background
Weight: Bucks 11 pounds

or over; Does 12 pounds or over

This distinctive breed was derived from the Flemish Giant and is an excellent exhibition rabbit. The first Checkered Giants were imported into the United States in 1910 and since that time, the breed has developed into a distinctive American type. The body is long and well arched, with medium-broad hindquarters. The butterfly across the nose, eye circles, cheek spots, ears, spine marking, tail, and side markings are clear and distinct.

CHINCHILLA
Breeds: American, Giant, and Standard
Color: To be like that of real Chinchilla
Undercolor is dark slate

Checkered Giants are one of the larger breeds of rabbits.

blue at the base, followed by a band of light pearl, followed by a band of black, then a light band ticked with black. The chest is pearl and the belly is white. All three breeds share this distinct color pattern, but each is considered a separate breed.

The Chinchilla produces the highest-priced rabbit pelt in Europe and is a prize exhibition rabbit.

AMERICAN CHINCHILLA: Bred for size, the American is the result of selectively breeding the Standard Chinchilla. It is medium in body length and well rounded in the hips, with well-filled loin and hips. The back is slightly arched starting at the ear base.

Weight: Bucks 9 to 11

Chinchillas have bright and glossy fur.

CINNAMON
Color: Rust or cinnamon; a

Weight: Bucks 8^1/$_2$ to 10^1/$_2$ pounds; Does 9 to 11 pounds

The Cinnamon is a rabbit of medium length. Both its hindquarters and shoulders are well developed. The smooth, well-rounded hindquarters, well filled with flesh are slightly wider and deeper than the shoulders and should blend into a well-

> "**The Chinchilla produces the highest-priced rabbit pelt....**"

pounds; Does 10 to 12 pounds

GIANT CHINCHILLA: The Giant came about by selective crossbreeding with Flemish Giants. This is the only giant rabbit that is considered primarily a meat type. The body is large, full in front and hindquarters, with a firm, meaty saddle.

Weight: Bucks 12 pounds and over; Does 13 pounds and over

STANDARD CHINCHILLA: The Standard Chinchilla's body is short and broad. In overall appearance, it appears compact.

Weight: Bucks 5 to 7 pounds; Does 5^1/$_2$ to 7^1/$_2$ pounds

darker color is to be present on all extremities

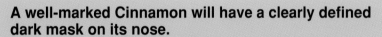

A well-marked Cinnamon will have a clearly defined dark mask on its nose.

The Creme D'Argent is a very pretty rabbit with distinguishing fur color.

rounded loin and back. The well-shaped head is to be in proportion to the body.

CREME D'ARGENT
    Color: Creamy orange
    Weight: Bucks 8 to $10^1/_2$ pounds; Does $8^1/_2$ to 11 pounds
    The Creme D'Argent is similar to the Champagne, but is smaller. It has a moderately long body with well-developed hindquarters, deep, thick loins, and broad, well-

BELOW: If you decide to breed rabbits at some point, they must be kept in very good physical condition.

developed shoulders. The back is slightly arched and tapers toward the shoulders. The color is creamy white with an orange cast. The undercolor is bright orange down to the skin.

DUTCH

Varieties: Black, Blue, Chocolate, Tortoise, Steel, and Gray

Weight: Bucks and Does, 3^1/$_2$ to 5^1/$_2$ pounds

The Dutch is the popular white rabbit with contrasting "britches." It is strictly a fancy or exhibition rabbit, with a very distinct color pattern. Although small, this breed is meaty, compact, and cobby.

DWARF HOTOT

Color: White throughout, except for the eyebands, which are black

Weight: Bucks and Does, 3^1/$_4$ pounds maximum

If you see a rabbit with dark eyebands, chances are it is a Dwarf Hotot.

The Dwarf Hotot is one of the newer additions to the rabbit fancy. Its body is short, compact, and well rounded. Hindquarters are well rounded and there is uniform width from shoulders to hips. The head is relatively large, with short, well-furred ears. The distinguishing feature of the breed is the black eyeband that outlines the eye. It should be narrow and uniform,

In an English Spot, both sides of the animal should be marked in the same way.

without and breaks or feathering.

ENGLISH SPOT

Varieties: Black, Blue, Chocolate, Gold, Gray, Lilac, and Tortoise

Color: Colored markings on a white background

Weight: Bucks and Does, 5 to 8 pounds

This is a very old breed imported from England. The face markings are similar to those of the Checkered Giant. The chain markings on the sides of the body run up to the base of the ears.

This chain is a very important part of the breed's markings

The Flemish Giant is the largest of all domestic breeds.

and should not appear on the Checkered Giant. As an exhibition rabbit, the English Spot's markings are of prime importance–not too few, not too many, not too small, not too large. A good specimen is a breeder's delight.

FLEMISH GIANT
Varieties: Steel Gray, Light Gray, Sandy, Black, Blue, White, and Fawn
Weight: Bucks 13 pounds or over; Does 14 pounds or over

This is probably one of the most popular of the giant breeds. It has one of the oldest and strongest recognized breed clubs in the United States. The Flemish Giant exhibits a powerful, massive build that is proportioned and well balanced throughout.

FLORIDA WHITE
Color: White
Weight: Bucks and Does, 4 to 6 pounds

The Florida White was

> **"The Flemish Giant is probably one of the most popular of the giant breeds."**

originally developed for research purposes. This is a rather short rabbit whose shoulders and hindquarters are well developed. The top line of the Florida White should be one that is curved, rising gradually from ear base to the center of the hips and then curving downward to the tail base. The Florida White has a round, full head, topped by stocky and well-furred ears. Both the head and the ears are to be in balance with the body.

HARLEQUIN
Groups: Japanese and Magpie
Varieties: Black, Blue, Chocolate, and Lilac
Weight: Bucks $6^1/_2$ to 9 pounds; Does 7 to $9^1/_2$ pounds

There are two types of Harlequin rabbit; the Japanese and the Magpie. The Japanese variety has its base coat color

The Flemish Giant is the largest of all domestic breeds.

Harlequins are noted for their checkered-pattern coloration.

Harlequins are very muscular rabbits.

alternating with bands of orange or its dilute. The Magpie has the basic color alternating with bands of white. This is much the same as a calico cat.

The head is divided in color, one side the base color, the other side the banding color of orange, its dilute, or white. The ears are to be the opposite color for each side, giving a checkered appearance. Also, the legs alternate in color.

HAVANA

Varieties: Blue, Chocolate, and Black

Weight: Bucks and Does, $4^1/_2$ to $6^1/_2$ pounds

The Havana is a small meaty rabbit. The body is cobby, with meaty

The Himalayan is long and cylindrical in shape.

Havanas are often used to improve the fur of other breeds.

shoulders tapering from slightly broader and higher hindquarters. The rich fur is soft and lustrous with a high sheen.

HIMALAYAN

Varieties: Black and Blue

Weight: Bucks and Does, $2^1/_2$ to $4^1/_2$ pounds

One of the world's oldest recognized breeds of rabbit. The coat is snow white with the nose, ears, feet, and tail a rich, velvety black or a rich medium blue at maturity. This is an exhibition rabbit with ruby-red eyes. Fanciers take care not to expose the coat to the sun, as the markings may fade to a gray or a rusty brown. Older specimens have a tendency to lose the rich color of this distinctively patterned coat, too.

HOTOT

Color: White throughout, except for the eyebands, which are deep black

Weight: Bucks 8 to 10 pounds; Does 9 to 11 pounds

This breed of rabbit is not quite as well known as are many of the other rabbit breeds. The Hotot's notable characteristic is the deep black band that encircles the eye, providing a striking contrast with the whiteness of the rest of the body.

In conformation, the Hotot is well rounded. Its musculation, which is easily distributed, imparts an impression of strength. An overall compactness is desirable in the breed.

JERSEY WOOLY

Groups: Agouti, Pointed White, Self, Shaded, Tan Pattern

Colors: Self–Black, Blue Chocolate, Lilac; Self–(Blue-eyed White and Ruby-Eyed White)–White; Shaded–Blue Cream, Sable Point, Seal,

A Dwarf Hotot.

Siamese Sable, Smoke Pearl, Tortoise; Agouti–Chestnut Agouti, Chinchilla, Opal, Squirrel; Tan Pattern–Black Otter, Black Silver Marten, Blue Silver Marten, Blue Otter, Chocolate Silver Marten, Lilac Silver Marten, Sable Silver Marten, Smoke Pearl Marten; Pointed (Pointed White)–White

Weight: Bucks and Does, 3$^{1}/_{2}$ pounds or under

The Jersey Wooly is another of the new wool rabbit breeds. It was developed by Bonnie Seeley. This small rabbit, whose pint-sized stature can be attributed, in part, to crossings with a Netherland Dwarf, sports a dense wool coat. However, the ears should not have large tufts or tassels. The ends of the ears may carry small tufts.

The Jersey Wooly's overall appearance is one of compactness and good depth.

The Jersey Wooly is available in an assortment of colors.

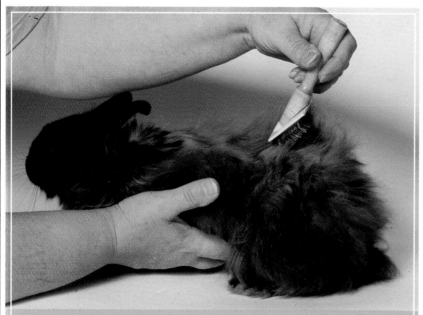

Key characteristics of the Lilac are its color and a dense, silky coat.

LILAC

Color: Dove-gray with a pinkish tint

Weight: Bucks $5^1/_2$ to $7^1/_2$ pounds; Does 6 to 8 pounds

The Lilac is a compact breed of rabbit that is robust and energetic in its overall appearance. Other physical qualities are those of balance and well roundedness. A good Lilac will radiate a warm glow, due to the pinkish-dove hue of the lustrous fur. In texture, the fur is both dense and soft to the touch.

LOP (ENGLISH)

Groups: Agouti, Brindled, Broken, Self, Shaded, Solid, Ticked

Weight:

Bucks 9 pounds and over; Does 10 pounds and over

The body of the English Lop is massive, thick set, and well fleshed. The outstanding feature of this breed is the ears which, when measured from tip to tip, should be at least 21 inches in length. The English Lop is considered to be one of the oldest domesticated-rabbit breeds. In Europe, it is sometimes referred to as the "King of the Fancy."

> "The body of the English Lop is massive, thick set, and well fleshed."

LOP (FRENCH)

Groups: Agouti, Brindled, Broken, Self, Shaded, Solid, Ticked

Weight: Bucks 10 pounds and over; Does 11 pounds

and over

The body is of medium length with the back well arched and the head carried low. In showing this breed, the ear carriage and the crown should suggest a horseshoe shape. Members of this breed are known for their friendly and affectionate natures.

LOP (HOLLAND)

Groups: Agouti, Broken, Pointed White, Self, Shaded, Solid, Ticked

Color: All colors within the recognized groups

Weight: Bucks and Does, not over 4 pounds

The most obvious feature of lop rabbits are their ears.

The Holland Lop is a solid and stocky little rabbit. In its general appearance, the animal is compact and balanced throughout. Ideally, the ears are to hang closely to the cheeks. They should be

Lop rabbits are known for their enormous ears.

On occasion, Holland Lops have been known to display a temper.

While ear length is important in English Lops, they all should have good quality and balance which is equally significant.

The Mini Lop was developed in Germany.

in balance with the rest of the body and with the head. The Holland Lop is known for its lively and inquisitive personality.

LOP (MINI)

Groups: Agouti, Broken, Pointed White, Self, Shaded, Solid, Ticked

Colors: All colors within the recognized groups

Weight: Bucks and Does, $4\frac{1}{2}$ to $6\frac{1}{2}$ pounds

The Mini Lop is thickset and solid. Its broad shoulders have good depth and are well filled. Compactness and balance are reflected in the animal's overall appearance. Mini Lop does are known for

Mini Lops are thickset and solid.

Mini Rex rabbits have a velvet-like coat.

"In general appearance, the Mini Rex is diminutive, balanced, and uniform throughout. "

A Mini Rex.

their good parental instincts.

MINI REX

Varieties: Blue, Californian, Castor, Chinchilla, Opal, Lynx, Red, Seal, Tortoise, White, Broken Group

Weight: Bucks 3 to $4^1/_4$ pounds; Does $3^1/_4$ to $4^1/_2$ pounds

In general appearance, the Mini Rex is diminutive, balanced, and uniform throughout. An ideal specimen of the breed will also be short in the body and well proportioned.

NETHERLAND DWARF

Groups: Self, Shaded, Agouti, Tan Pattern, Any Other Variety

Colors: Selfs–White, Black, Blue, Chocolate, Lilac; Shaded–Siamese Sable, Siamese Smoke Pearl, Sable Point; Agouti-Chinchilla, Lynx, Opal,

Squirrel, Chestnut; Tan Pattern–Sable Marten, Silver Marten, Smoke Pearl Marten, Otter, Tans; Any Other Variety–Fawn, Himalayan, Orange, Steel, Tortoiseshell

Weight: Bucks and Does, not over $2^1/_2$ pounds

The Netherland Dwarf is the smallest of all the breeds of rabbit and has the greatest variety of colors and patterns. It is an imported breed from the Netherlands, and its popularity has grown steadily. Not since the days of importation of the Belgian Hare has any one breed so caught the attention of the fancy.

The Netherland Dwarf

The Netherland Dwarf is the smallest rabbit breed in the world.

Netherland Dwarfs will consume less food compared to other breeds.

New Zealands
are bred
mainly for
their meat.

has a short, compact,
cobby body with wide
shoulders. The coat is
dense and the ears are
rather small in comparison
to body size.

NEW ZEALAND
Varieties: Black, Red,
and White
Weight: Bucks 9 to 11
pounds; Does 10 to 12
pounds
The New Zealand is
considered to be the all-
purpose rabbit-bred for
meat, fur, show, and
laboratory use. The
appearance suggests good
balance and uniformity,
with the body well-fleshed.
The body should be
medium in length and have
good depth and width,
suggesting a solid animal.

PALOMINO
Varieties: Golden and
Lynx
Weight: Bucks 8 to 10
pounds; Does 9 to 11
pounds
This is a breed developed
in the United States to be
equal to the New Zealand in

**New Zealand rabbits can
come in three color
varieties.**

The Palomino was developed in the United States.

REX
Varieties: Black, Black Otter, Blue, Californian, castor, Chinchilla, Chocolate, Lilac, Lynx, Opal, Red, Sable, Seal, White, Broken Group

Weight: Bucks $7^1/_2$ to $9^1/_2$ pounds; Does 8 to $10^1/_2$ pounds

This breed was developed from a mutation of the normal-coated rabbit. Unlike normal rabbit fur, with its longer guard hairs, the Rex coat has no conspicuous guard hairs. They are present, but are of the same length as the undercoat. The breed is well proportioned with a medium-length body having good depth and well-rounded hips. It is filled out in the loins, typical of meat-type rabbits.

RHINELANDER
Color: White with markings of black and bright golden-orange

Weight: Bucks $6^1/_2$ to $9^1/_2$ pounds; Does 7 to 10

quality and to be attractive in color. As in all utility rabbits, the Palomino has a body that is well fleshed. The back has a gradual arch so as to appear rounded in the back, loin, and hindquarters.

The Golden variety is an attractive shade of gold with cream or white undercolor. The Lynx variety has a pearl-gray surface coloration that blends into the intermediate coloration of orange/beige. The undercolor appears light cream to white.

POLISH
Varieties: Black, Blue, Chocolate, Blue-eyed White, Ruby-eyed White

Weight: Bucks and Does, not over $3^1/_2$ pounds

This is a popular exhibition rabbit. It is raised strictly for show, and fanciers have developed a Blue-Eyed White and a Ruby-Eyed White, which

are shown as separate varieties.

The body is small and compact with well-rounded hips. The short fur is fine and dense. It is fly-back and lies medium close to the body. The head is medium full, short, and has a slight curvature in the skull from ear to nose.

Be wary of Polish breeds for they could have lively temperaments.

The coat of Rex rabbits has guard hairs that are the same length as the undercoat.

pounds

In general appearance, the Rhinelander's body is rounded and closely resembles a cylindrical shape. The length of the animal should be such that it gives the appearance of grace. The Rhinelander projects an overall impression of attentiveness and vivacity.

The well-shaped head, which is set closely on the shoulders, should be in balance with the body.

SATIN

Varieties: Black, Blue, Californian, Chinchilla, Chocolate, Copper, Red, Siamese, White, and

Rhinelanders typically exhibit well-rounded proportions.

Satins are very popular and come in a variety of colors.

Broken Group

Weight: Bucks $8^1/_2$ to $10^1/_2$ pounds; Does 9 to 11 pounds

Developed in the United States, the Satin is distinguishable by the beautiful sheen of its fur. The quality of the Satin's fur is the result of a mutation.

In overall appearance, the Satin is of medium length, with rather short legs. The Satin has its own standard by which its fur is judged.

All Satins have erect ears.

Silver rabbits are commonly seen in shows.

Silver Fox rabbit.

SILVER

Varieties: Black, Brown, Fawn

Weight: Bucks and Does, 4 to 7 pounds

This is another of the fancy breeds, bred mainly for show. The body is plump with good loins and firm flesh. It gives a handsome appearance. Color is of prime importance, with the top color as silvery as possible and ticked with white throughout the entire body, head, ears, and feet.

The colors of the Silver's undercolor are a deep blue in the Black variety, chestnut-brown in the Brown variety, and a rich orange shade in the Fawn variety.

"The Silver Fox is a large, meaty breed."

SILVER FOX

Varieties: Blue and Black and Chocolate.

Weight: Bucks 9 to 11 pounds; Does 10 to 12 pounds

This is a large, meaty breed. The body is broad, meaty, and slightly arched. It has a deep loin and is

If properly cared for, your rabbit should live between six to eight years. Some have even lived past twelve years.

medium in length with medium bone. The most unique feature about this rabbit is its long, silvery coat, which resembles fox fur.

SILVER MARTEN

Varieties: Black, Blue, Chocolate, Sable

Weight: Bucks $6^1/2$ to $8^1/2$ pounds; Does $7^1/2$ to $9^1/2$ pounds

This breed is a sport (mutation) from the Chinchilla. The unique appearance of the fur is due to silver-tipped guard hairs. In developing the Chinchilla breed, a black Tan was introduced. The Silver Marten is silver in those areas where the black Tan is tan. In England, this breed is known as the Silver Fox rabbit.

TAN

Varieties: Black, Blue, Chocolate, Lilac

Weight: Bucks 4 to $5^1/2$ pounds; Does 4 to 6 pounds

It is believed that the original Black and Tan rabbits were sports from the mating between a wild rabbit and a Dutch. The markings of the Tan rabbit are a stable genetic feature. The body color is solid, free of white hairs. The tan markings should be rich and bright. They appear on the triangle that encircles the neck, the inner part of the front and hind legs, the chest, belly, flanks, eye circles, inside edges of the ears, and underside of the tail. The body of the tan is compact and slightly arched.

Silver Martens are the result of a cross between a Chinchilla and a Tan rabbit.

Tan rabbits get their name from their tan undercolor.

Note the deep, rich color on this Tan rabbit.

The biggest decision you will make when choosing a rabbit is selecting one that would best be suited to your household.

BREEDING BETTER RABBITS

Breeding rabbits is educational, fascinating, and enjoyable. Since rabbits reproduce so rapidly and many generations of them can be produced in a lifetime of man, they are excellent subjects for studying the results of different breeding programs. Every characteristic, from color of fur to color of eye, from size to carriage of ear, is controlled by genes, minute units of coded information that are passed on from one individual to another through inheritance.

At some point, you might become interested in mating your rabbit to obtain cute young. This does not only require breeding experience, but relevant information about the biological regularities in the reproduction of rabbits. Such processes are particularly valuable for children which can gain reliable experiences for events in home and garden and a useful appreciation of the natural environment.

Sexual maturity in rabbits is reached at an age of three months. Males will form the first fully developed sperm in about 4 months. However, it would be wrong to use the animals at that age already for breeding. Females should be at least 5, preferably 6 months old at the onset of breeding. it is not advisable to use bucks for breeding prior to seventh months of age. If the animals are younger than that, there is a real danger of too much physiological strain. This is notably true in females. Premature birth would be common and females which are too young have problems raising their young.

The domestic rabbit does not have a regular oestrus. Release of the egg is triggered by copulation. Following the introduction of the sperm, about 10 hours after copulation, ovulation commences.

Since maternal egg cells are viable for up to 8 hours and paternal sperm for 30 to 32

> ## "Sexual maturity in rabbits is reached at an age of three months."

hours, fertilization occurs in the oviduct, to where the spermatozoans have

If you choose to breed rabbits, it is advisable to purchase stock with minor defects from excellent specimens.

advanced, provided there are no malfunctions. A single copulation can produce up to 400 million spermatozoans.

The biology of heredity is called genetics. Genetics is the coming together of genes. Genes can be either dominant or recessive. A gene that masks the

characteristic of another gene is said to to be dominant. The gene that is masked is termed recessive. The dominant genes will show themselves in the young, while the recessive ones will be carried and may or may not show themselves. Only when two recessives come together will the recessive trait make itself known. Such is the case of buck teeth or splay legs. If an individual in a litter of otherwise healthy and normal baby rabbits has either of these traits, it has inherited a recessive gene for the condition from each parent. The rest of the litter may be carrying this recessive gene to pass on to their young, or they may be clear.

There are three types of breeding programs. They are known as inbreeding, linebreeding, and outcrossing. Inbreeding is the mating of closely related animals. This can be the mating of littermate to littermate, father to daughter, or mother to son. It is the quickest method for setting a type, as the young will possess a uniform likeness and similar genetic makeup. With inbreeding, both desirable and undesirable traits can be passed on to future generations. The use of inbreeding will quickly reveal if certain animals are worthy of breeding at all. If the majority of the young are good, they are worth reproducing. If the majority

A pair of rabbits mating.

are only fair or poor, it is better not to inbreed.

Linebreeding is the mating of closely related animals to maintain a high relationship to a particular ancestor. By selecting a highly desirable ancestor and breeding-related individuals that possess the same traits, the young will carry many of the genes of that ancestor. Examples of linebreeding are the mating of nephew to aunt, cousin to cousin, and uncle to niece.

Outcrossing is the mating of unrelated individuals. Outcrossing is unpredictable, as one never knows which recessive, or hidden genes are carried. As many faults as good qualities can be introduced into stock by this method. Outcrossing is used when first starting out or when one has inbred or linebred until it is desirable to bring in new genes. Even then, it is more predictable to bring in a distant relative from another line.

It is important to know that copulation should take

place in surroundings familiar to the male, since a female will not be in a position there to defend any territorial rights. This makes her more accessible to the male. Copulation can be attempted whether the female shows any readiness to mate or not. Usually, the females will show no readiness until it is in the presence of a male. The smell of the male, and when he licks her head and neck, stimulates the

> "However, some females are so stubborn and resistant that the male cannot copulate properly."

female sufficiently so that there are usually no problems to achieve a satisfactory copulation. If, for some reason

copulation does not take place immediately, the female should be left in an empty male cage, and after a few hours it usually comes into heat. Moreover, oats, fed in slightly larger portions a few days prior to the planned copulation can act as an "aphrodisiac." However, some females are so stubborn and resistant that the male cannot copulate properly. There is no point continuing with mating attempts since the males will be unnecessarily weakened by the continuous efforts or it may even be injured by an aggressive female. Moreover, young bucks often fail because of inexperience.

After copulation has been completed, the female remains in position with her rear raised slightly and the buck slides away from the

To produce young rabbits, you will need to find a suitable pair.

female omitting soft growling noises. You must not be alarmed when the male then suddenly lies down briefly in what appears to be some sort of a convulsion. This is quite a natural behavior. A single copulation is usually sufficient. The number of mature eggs already in the oviduct at the time of copulation is enough for achieving fertilization, not repeated copulation.

A pregnancy may be indicated when the female moves about restlessly and starts to scratch around in the straw, a few days later. The pregnant animal must then be isolated. She must be protected against further advances by the male. If there are then no further signs of pregnancy and when the projected date of birth passes, a renewed copulation can be attempted. A rabbit's gestation period is generally between 28 and 31 days.

If the female displays changes in her behavior during the weeks after copulation, it is quite probable that she is pregnant. Females that have been rather temperamental all along suddenly become noticeably quieter, others may become aggressive and will even bite. Females must be given a lot of peace and quiet. Ideally, the animal should be left in a spacious cage or outdoor hutch where it can prepared for the birth of her young.

When the pregnant female is close to full term, she will start to build a nest. For that purpose, she gathers hay and straw and even pulls out some

of her own fur to line the nest's interior. If birth occurs prior to the 28th day, the young are usually dead at birth or will die soon after. Similarly, birth significantly beyond the 31st day will often produce dead young. These must be

The male and female reproductive organs of rabbits.

removed from the nest quickly. It should be kept in mind that lactating females often resent such human intervention. Some animals will scratch and bite, so that we have to select an opportune moment when she is not sitting on or near the nest. Sometimes, it is also possible to coax the animal away from the nest with some tempting food morsel, which gives us enough time to open the nest material slightly to determine the condition of the young.

Rabbits usually give birth to four to five young, but a litter may also contain up to six of seven young. The young are typically naked and blind. Consequently, they need warmth from their mother who must also nurse them. The female must not

be disturbed while she is nursing her young, no matter how curious we are to see the baby rabbits.

It is possible that a female will not nurse her own young rabbits. the reason for this could have been difficulties during birth or the animal is simply too young for her maternal instincts to have properly developed yet. When there have been nutritional deficiencies or when a female was frightened during birth, some may then become cannibalistic. When this happens with a litter, the next one from such female is usually reared without difficulties.

Normally, a nursing female will rear her young and care for them during the next 6 weeks after birth. Keepers can help her efforts by feeding at regular intervals on time and by giving a variable diet as well as always having her water available. Nursing females are always thirsty. After 6 weeks, the young can be taken away from their mother. If any or all of the young are not to be kept, they should be left for another three weeks in their familiar surroundings, and should only be given away once they are sufficiently strong.

HOUSING

The primary factors to consider when planning housing for rabbits are climate, comfort, and sanitation. The more thought and planning that you put into the housing of the rabbit that you keep, the less work and expense there will be for you. Many pet shops stock cages, as well as other kinds of supplies, that are specially designed for rabbits. Although metal cages may seem an unnecessary expense when compared to a wood hutch or cardboard box, the rabbits will fare much better. Wood hutches are fine, but in the long run they become unsanitary and are difficult to clean. There is no need to go into detail about the cardboard box.

You should never attempt to pick up a rabbit by the ears.

Once the bottom is urine soaked or the rabbit chews its way out, the box will have to be thrown away. No matter what type of cage that you choose, the floor should provide solid footing and, at the same time, allow waste material to fall through.

Good hygiene is one of the essential elements of good husbandry and should be reflected in all aspects of care, from cleaning to feeding to grooming. Your pet's cage should be thoroughly cleaned on a weekly basis. If you decide to keep more than one rabbit, you may have to increase the frequency of cage cleaning. Food and water bowls or bottles should be cleaned as well. Any feeding utensils that become chipped or cracked should be thrown away.

The dimensions for hutches or cages vary with the size of the rabbit breed. A cage to house a breed of medium size is 18 inches high and 36 inches wide by 30 inches long. For the giant breeds, 36 inches by 60 inches or up to 72 inches by 24 inches is preferred, and small breeds need only 24 inches by 24 inches by 18 inches high. Hutches may be constructed of wood and wire mesh. If the hutch is made entirely of wire mesh, they may be set on wooden legs or suspended by wires from the ceiling of a building. Since the worst hazards to rabbits are cold winds and high temperatures, the cages should be protected from sunshine in the summer and wind and rain in the

winter.

In mild climates, cages may be placed out of doors in a shaded area or provided with shade by means of an open-end

Proper housing is vital if you expect your rabbit to live a long, healthy life.

Rabbits need plenty of room and plenty of exercise. If this is not provided, they will become muscle-bound.

building. In more severe climates, the rabbits should be housed indoors with good ventilation. The addition of heat in winter is an asset. If no heat is available, lights may be suspended above the nest boxes to warm the young. In the summer, heat prostration is the greatest threat to raising healthy rabbits. Not only do rabbits die if overheated or if allowed to remain in the sun without protection, but also the buck will become temporarily sterile when the temperature remains above 90 degrees for

over 30 days.

Nest boxes in a variety of designs are available for purchase. The average size is 8 inches high and 18 inches long by 12 inches wide. However, the size of the breed should be considered. There should always be room enough for the doe to turn around in the box, but enough room to encourage remaining in the nest when her duties of caring for the young are complete. One side must be low enough to allow the doe to enter without damage to herself by striking the edge as she leaps in or out.

Cardboard boxes are poor examples for a rabbit's living accommodations.

Regular cleaning of cages and nest boxes is crucial for sanitation. After weaning each litter, the boxes are cleaned by washing with water and a disinfectant, scrubbing with a brush, then drying in the sun. They are then stored and ready for the next litter.

Rabbits select a corner of the cage to be used as a toilet, and although wire mesh is used, the droppings do not always fall through and will accumulate in that corner. Scraping the wire bottom or hosing it before it becomes heavily soiled will keep the

A wire cage provides durable housing for your rabbit.

cage clean. The build-up of hair can also pose a problem if not removed periodically. Most commercial rabbitries use a torch to burn it away, but a hose can be used satisfactorily. It is a good idea to keep several empty cages on hand. The rabbits can then be rotated into these cages while their own quarters are being cleaned. If the rabbit keeper works frequently with his animals and handles them in a calm manner, they will be gentle and easy to care for. Also, the small problems that arise can be checked before they become large ones.

FEEDING

A good diet is reflected by your rabbit's fur.

Rabbits are herbivores. In other words, they only eat vegetable matter. Their relatives out in the wild sustain themselves mainly on grasses and various other kinds of vegetation. The pet rabbit is dependent on his owner for a diet that will meet his nutritional needs and help keep him healthy. There are a number of important elements in a rabbit's diet that must be offered in the proper ratio if the animal's metabolic requirements are to be met. They include proteins, carbohydrates, fats, vitamins, and minerals.

If you are like most people believing that rabbits eat plenty of lettuce, cabbage, and carrots, you couldn't be more wrong. Nutritionists see it differently. These experts have concluded that rabbits require a balanced diet to grow and reproduce. There are plenty of things that a rabbit will eat, cabbage, lettuce, and carrots included. Nevertheless, if you want your rabbit to be happy, you should feed him what he should eat. His

quality roughage, special sources of protein, phosphorus and calcium which are essential trace minerals, and sources of necessary vitamins. The protein levels of these pellets range from 16 to 20 percent, the higher number necessary for the growing young rabbit, the lower needed as a "maintenance" diet for the adult rabbit.

If all you ever give your rabbit is pellets to eat and clean water to drink, you and he will be doing fine. In spite of all the evidence

under any circumstances. They won't do any good and can kill them. It's the drastic change in diet that causes this. Consistency is the key to a rabbit's diet. Rabbit pellets work best because they contain everything that a rabbit needs in a single pellet.

As you feed a young

> **"Never give any greens, such as carrots, lettuce, or cabbage, to rabbits less than six months of age under any circumstances."**

nutritional future is in your hands.

A rabbit keeper doesn't have to be an expert in nutrition to feed his pet properly. The key to a good rabbit diet is very simple– pelleted rabbit food. These specially formulated food mixes, developed by experts in animal nutrition, provide all of the dietary essentials that your rabbit needs. You should check with your vet to determine the formula that is best for your rabbit.

Your pet store should have rabbit pellets in stock. If you own just one rabbit, then it makes sense to buy a few fresh pounds at a time from your local petshop. These pellets contain alfalfa hay for high-

that pellets are the best feed for rabbits, there are those who insist upon feeding them other things. That's when they get into trouble and when their rabbits get sick. It should be pointed out that rabbits can exist and even thrive on other feeds, although the chances are that they won't.

Water is an important part of your rabbit's diet. A rabbit should have access to clean fresh water at all times. If you use a water bottle, be sure that it is not placed directly above the food bowl.

Never give any greens, such as carrots, lettuce, or cabbage, to rabbits less than six months of age

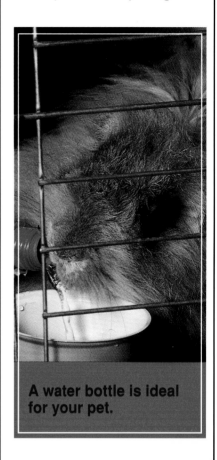

A water bottle is ideal for your pet.

rabbit all the rabbit pellets he can eat in a day, you will soon find out how much that is. A lot depends on the size and age of your rabbit. If he leaves some pellets uneaten, give less on the following day. If your rabbit greets you at feeding time by trying to tear the door off his cage to get at your feed sack, you will want to give him more.

Adult rabbits of the

medium-weight group eat about five ounces per day. Again, more or less, depending upon the individual. You may ask yourself, how much precisely should I feed my rabbit to make sure he gets enough but not too much. There's no exact answer, but there is some practical advice. You should keep a close watch on your rabbit, particularly at feeding time. Run your hand over your rabbit. If he's a bit bony, give him more. If he hasn't cleaned up his pellets, you are probably giving too much, so feed less.

The first thing to check when you find that your rabbit is not eating enough is his water supply. A rabbit that is thirsty will not eat dry rabbit pellets. He needs water at all times. Secondly, note his droppings. They should be large and dry and round. If a rabbit is not eating well but is apparently healthy, try

Pelleted food formulated especially for rabbits is the most important part of a rabbit's diet. It can be purchased in various sizes and packages to meet the needs of the individual rabbit owner. Photo courtesy of Hagen.

tempting him with a piece of dry bread or a spoonful of oatmeal.

You never want to forget to feed your rabbit every day and at the same time every day. The evening is the best time of day to feed rabbits because rabbits are more active then than during the daylight hours. If you would like to feed your rabbit twice a day, you could divide the pellets into evening and morning feedings. But one feeding a day is plenty.

"...you could divide the pellets into evening and morning feedings."

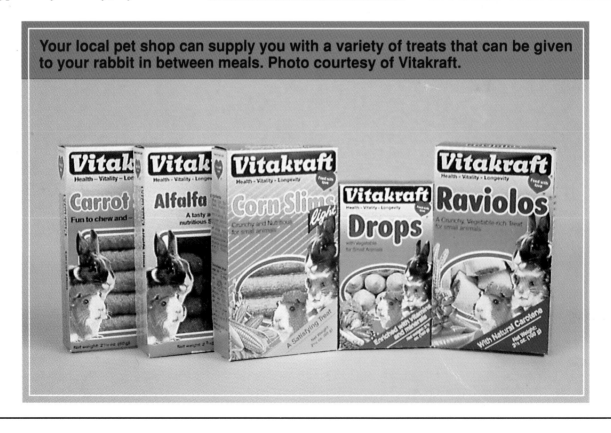

Your local pet shop can supply you with a variety of treats that can be given to your rabbit in between meals. Photo courtesy of Vitakraft.